POETRY ON THE BUSES

Poetry
on the
Buses

edited by Candy Neubert and Valerie Belsey

Green Books

First published in 2001
by Green Books Ltd
Foxhole, Dartington
Totnes, Devon TQ9 6EB

Cover design by Rick Lawrence
Tel: 01803 840956

Text printed by Bell & Bain Ltd, Glasgow

British Library Cataloguing in Publication Data
available on request

ISBN 1 903998 03 4

Contents

The only way to be sure of catching a bus
is to miss the one before it.

adapted from G. K. Chesterton

Introduction

If you're trying to memorise that poem you saw on a bus this morning, here's the solution: *Poetry on the Buses* is a one-way ticket to taking the complete collection home with you. This is a collection of poems for everyone—especially for those who have chosen to leave their cars at home.

Like the founders of the Poems on the Underground scheme, we have no hidden agenda in publishing this book, although by adding that 'something' to a bus ride we are encouraging you to take the bus—not the car.

Choosing the poems seemed a simple enough task—and what a pleasure. Seeing the first ten transformed into narrow, vinyl posters confirmed what we'd already guessed—that we would have to use very short ones. Long blocks of words would be difficult to read from a sitting position on a moving bus. Eight lines had to be the maximum, six or four lines being even better. This (literally) narrowed the choice enormously: some poets haven't written anything of eight lines or less. Having said that, there are a few longer poems in the collection, which were selected for use on bus shelters.

We wanted to leave out poems already anthologized, to give lesser poets an airing. With only one poem per poet, we tried to cast the net as widely as possible, wanting to include some classics, household names, unknowns, the ancient, the new, the anonymous, the foreign, the funny and (it couldn't help creeping in) those which seemed particular to riding on a bus.

Many of the poems are out of copyright, but we're especially grateful to those writers who gave us permission to use their work for no fee at all. May they have lasting fame for travelling that extra mile.

There was another component to add: a need to involve the general public. We asked for contributions, sending out word through libraries, post offices and newspapers, wondering if this would bring any replies or vanish into the black hole of literary submissions. There were hundreds of replies. Despite their variety and our different tastes, we miraculously made our choice without coming to blows.

The project started with a small grant from a local council to put up poems on buses and bus shelters in Devon, our local area. Soon we had Green Books with us, and a plan to publish. We're now delighted to have another partner in this project: Arriva, who are donating advertising space on their buses.

We hope that these poems will help you make the most of your bus journeys. Maybe someone, somewhere, will be waiting for their next bus and thinking, *I wonder if there's a poem on it?*

Candy Neubert
Valerie Belsey

The Ptarmigan

The ptarmigan is strange,
As strange as he can be;
Never sits on ptelephone poles
Or roosts upon a ptree.
And the way he ptakes pto spelling
Is the strangest thing pto me.

Anon

The Little Car

31st August 1914

And when having passed that afternoon
Through Fontainebleau
We arrived in Paris
Just as the mobilization posters were going up
We understood my buddy and I
That the little car had taken us into a New Epoch
And although we were both grown men
We had just been born.

Guillaume Apollinaire

Mice and Books

Prithee mice, begone and find
Richer cupboards, where cheese-rind
And dried raisins offer fare
Daintier than I can spare;
Such a shameless rioting
With my books, is not a thing
To indulge in—O be wise,
Do not nibble at them twice.

Ariston

Below the surface-stream

Below the surface-stream,
     Shallow and light,
Of what we *say* we feel—below the stream,
As light, of what we *think* we feel—there flows
With noiseless current strong, obscure and deep,
The central stream of what we feel indeed.

Matthew Arnold

The Life of Man

And one of the King's chief men presently said:

"It is as if thou wert sitting at a feast with
thy chief men and thy thanes in the winter-time:
and the hail is warmed, and outside it rains and
snows and storms.

Comes a sparrow and flies swiftly through one
Door and goes out another.

So is the life of man revealed for a brief space,
But what went before and what follows after
We know not."

The Venerable Bede

Catshapes

The geometrically
striped swirls.
which ripple round
this tiger's body
are renewed daily   as he stalks

                     tops
hedge

pawing up and sucks in
dewy, circling spidery webs.
Lessons in nature's geometry
digested then spun
on the spindle of his body.

Valerie Belsey

When a man has married a wife, he finds out whether
Her knees and elbows are only glued together.

William Blake

Stanza

I'll walk where my own nature would be leading:
  It vexes me to choose another guide:
Where the grey flocks in ferny glens are feeding;
  Where the wild wind blows on the mountainside.

Charlotte Brontë

In Freiburg Station

There is one memory God can never break,
There is one splendour more than all the pain,
There is one secret that shall never die,
Star-crowned I stand and sing, for that hour's sake.
In Freiburg station, waiting for a train,
I saw a Bishop with puce gloves go by.

Rupert Brooke

Green languid liquid cliff tops
slipping into calm blue sea,
meeting
feet thumping path to seagulls' cry.
Inside me all gorse coconut scent inviting
demanding
I glide subside and crumble as the cliff-tops.

Carola Buhse

The giant hornbill—
mostly a beak resembling
bananas—loves them.

Anthony Burge

On Rough Roads

I'm now arrived—thanks to the Gods!—
   Through pathways rough and muddy:
A certain sign that makin' roads
   Is no this people's study.

Yet, though I'm no wi' scripture crammed,
   I'm sure the Bible says
That heedless sinners shall be damn'd
   Unless they mend their ways.

Robert Burns

There is a pleasure in the pathless woods,
there is a rapture on the lonely shore,
there is a society where none intrudes
by the deep sea, and music in its roar.
I love not Man the less, but Nature more.

Lord Byron

Song of the road

Again let us dream where the land lies sunny
And live, like the bees, on our hearts' old honey,
Away from the world that slaves for money—
    Come, journey the way with me.

Madison Cawein

Song

I looked on the eyes o' fair woman too long
Till silence and shame stole the use o' my tongue
When I tried to speak to her I'd nothing to say
So I turned myself round and she wandered away
When she got too far off—why, I'd something to tell
So I sent sighs behind her and talked to mysel'.

John Clare

Van Gogh

Dark winds haunt the poplars,
a wild sun gyrates.
All the stars of heaven
blaze at one time.
But which time is it?

Valerie Clarke

All Nature seems at work. Slugs leave their lair—
The bees are stirring—birds are on the wing—
And Winter slumbering in the open air,
Wears on his smiling face a dream of Spring!
And I the while, the sole unbusy thing,
Nor honey make nor pair, nor build, nor sing.

Samuel Taylor Coleridge

There is nothing ugly; *I never saw an ugly thing in my life,* for let the form of an object be what it may—light, shade, and perspective will always make it beautiful.

John Constable

Buffalo

I went to the zoo and sat by a fence,
right near the head of a sleeping buffalo,
I sat there for a long time while he slept.

His head was massive, warm and heavy.
He shuffled a little in his sleep.
I sat by him until I was still as a prairie and wide.

He showed me some mystery and wildness
and that he still had his dreams.

Rose Cook

Extract from The Solitude of Alexander Selkirk

But the seafowl is gone to her nest,
The beast is laid down in his lair;
Even here is a season of rest,
And I to my cabin repair.
There's mercy, encouraging thought!
Gives even affliction a grace
And reconciles man to his lot.

William Cowper

Marble Arch

In war you'd hear a weary shout,
"Get off the bus there's bombs about".
Tired to the bone, we'd sigh and moan
As overhead an aircraft droned.
Our homeward journey interrupted
By boys killing as instructed.
We had become immune to fear
As we waited for the loud 'all clear'.

Pauline Crease

Extract from 'Journey'

My leather jacket
Soft as a highwayman's coat.
My money, its life.

John Daniel

Few among men are they who cross to the further shore.
The others merely run up and down the bank on this side.

From the *Dhammapada*

Exultation is the going
of an inland soul to sea,
past the houses—past the headlands—
into deep eternity—

Bred as we, among the mountains,
can the sailor understand
the divine intoxication
of the first league out from land?

Emily Dickinson

On a frosty night
The scent of last year's sunshine
Lies in clean blankets

Edna Eglinton

Beneath a tree
Crocus, petal bluish-white,
A thousand in a dozen rings
Gas-jets, ignite

Suddenly the kettle of
A blackbird
Sings.

David Farnsworth

Love amongst the Middle-aged

(For Nicky after 11323 blissful mornings)

Each morn at dawn the slanting light,
Romantic in my failing sight,
Surrounds, like love, her perfect form.

She moves about our nuptial dorm
And murmurs as in deep despair;
'Whatever is a girl to wear?'

I watch with tea cup in my grip,
Its rim obscures my trembling lip,
And realize how much I'm blessed:

Awakening from a long night's rest
To witness, freed from lust's blind curse,
My daily striptease in reverse.

Gus Ferguson

Tenebris Interlucentem

A linnet who had lost her way
Sang on a blackened bough in hell,
Till all the ghosts remembered well
The trees, the wind, the golden day.

At last they knew that they had died
When they heard music in that land,
And someone there stole forth a hand
To draw a brother to his side.

James Elroy Flecker

Folk song

When the chicken's in the eggshell, there is no bone;
When the cherry's in the blossom, there is no stone;
When the Bible's in the press, no man can read it;
When the wool is on the sheep's back, there is no thread.

All life is but a wandering to find home,
When we're gone, we're there.

John Ford

Everything is hidden.
At the hairdressers
behind my silvered image
the hand mirror swings
with black shoulders
like someone
playing hide-and-seek.
I think of you.

Berta R. Freistadt

Ghosts and Shadows

Ghosts in these forest shadows
Thrown back by night
Or in daylight
   like bats that drink from our veins
   and hang from moist walls, in deep caves
Behind this green moss, these awful white stones
We pray to know who has seen them
   Shadows thrown back by the night.

Gabon Pygmy

Park and Ride

He chose the park to tell her
public place less chance of a scene
left her sitting on a bench and drove away for ever
suddenly seeing
as he went
a blaze of tulips in the rearview mirror.

Jenny Galton-Fenzi

Chi non esce dal suo paese, vive pieno di preguidizi

He who never leaves his country is full of prejudices

Carlo Goldoni

She clicks the keys of the morning

Her world is mostly in her head
as she clicks the keys of the morning.
Cold toast and kisses, body fed,
her world is mostly in her head.
Abstruse perfection, someone said,
with mind alive and body yawning.
Her world is mostly in her head
as she clicks the keys of the morning.

Ronnie Goodyer

Ode on the Death of a Favourite Cat, Drowned in a Tub of Gold Fishes

From hence, ye Beauties undeceiv'd.
Know, one false step is ne'er retriev'd,
   And be with caution bold.
Not all that tempts your wand'ring eyes
And heedless hearts, is lawful prize;
   Nor all that glisters, gold.

Thomas Gray

The Epigram

Two lines of epigram exhaust their topic;
With one line more, the thing becomes an epic.

Grillus

The Garden Seat

Its former green is blue and thin,
And its once firm legs sink in and in:
Soon it will break down unaware,
Soon it will break down unaware.

At night when reddest flowers are black
Those who once sat thereon come back;
Quite a row of them sitting there,
Quite a row of them sitting there.

With them the seat does not break down,
Nor winter freeze them, nor floods drown,
For they are as light as upper air,
They are as light as upper air!

Thomas Hardy

Against writers that carp at other men's books

The readers and the hearers like my books,
And yet some writers cannot them digest;
But what care I? For when I make a feast,
I would my guests should praise it, not the cooks.

Sir J. Harington

Such Bus As Dreams Are Made Of

Your face is like the back end of a bus.
No, do not take offence, for none is meant.
It is intended as a compliment.
If you would just calm down and hush your fuss
I'll tell you, if I can, just how the view
Of that rear end of bus as it pulls out
From the bus-stop or rounds a roundabout,
Can fill my throbbing head with thoughts of you:
      Yours is the face that I've been waiting for,
      But when I try to catch you you've just been
      And gone. I'd travel, if I could afford it,
      To your sweet terminus, I'd pay that fare,
      Yet you elude me still
                  —See what I mean?
      Plus: you have advertising on your forehead.

Matt Harvey

Distich

What is a first love worth except to prepare for a second?
What does the second love bring? Only regret for the past.

John Milton Hay

Discontents in Devon

More discontents I never had
Since I was born, than here;
Where I have been, and still am sad,
In this dull Devon-shire.

Robert Herrick

I remember, I remember
the fir trees dark and high;
I used to think their slender tops
were close against the sky.
It was a childish ignorance,
but now 'tis little joy
to know I'm farther off from heaven
than when I was a boy.

Thomas Hood

He is so young, my child,
He cannot know the track.
O Guide from that strange world,
Hearken, I'll pay thee, but
Take him upon thy back.

From the Japanese, author unknown

Viewed from a train in Spain

Alondras de otros pueblos cantan en los trigales,
Skylarks from other villages sing in the wheat fields

su sangre transparente mecen las amapolas,
their clear blood gently rocking the poppies

y la hierba en los belfos, lentas vacas pintadas
and the hay in store. Painted in the meadows the slow cows

vuelven hacia nosotros sus testas melancólicas
turn their melancholy heads our way.

Juan Ramon Jimenez

Song

Give me a look, give me a face,
That makes simplicity a grace;
Robes loosely flowing, hayre as free:
Such sweet neglect more taketh me,
Than all th'adulteries of Art;
They strike mine eyes, but not my heart.

Ben Jonson

To love a man without return
Is to offer a prayer
To a devil's back
In a huge temple.

Lady Kasa

Dawlish Fair

Over the Hill and over the Dale,
  And over the Bourne to Dawlish
Where ginger-bread wives have a scanty sale,
  And ginger-bread nuts are smallish.

John Keats

The reality of eagles

Nothing can prepare us for eagles,
the reality of them,
their indifference,
the grandeur of their wings,
how they subjugate the air
and the space between mountains,
their shadows hovering
between us and the sun.

Angela Kirby

Ultimate Reality

A young man said to me:
I am interested in the problem of
                              Reality.

I said: Really!
Then I saw him turn to glance
                    surreptitiously,
In the big mirror, at his own
                    fascinating shadow.

D. H. Lawrence

Extract from the Enquiry

All Matter lives, and shews its Maker's Power
There's not a Seed but what contains a Flower:

When for blue Plumbs our longing Palate calls,
Or scarlet Cherries that adorn the Walls;
With each plump Fruit we swallow down a Tree.

Mary Leapor

The Roadside Pool

Drink not here, traveller, from this warm pool
In the brook, full of mud stirred by the sheep
At pasture; but go a very little way over the ridge
Where heifers are grazing; for there by yonder
Pastoral stone-pine thou wilt find bubbling through
The fountained rock a spring colder than northern snow.

Leonidas of Tarentum

The Steeple

Day and the enamelled colours of fall
fold into silhouette.
Tonight the moon will be blue in its fullness.
We will watch frost make a path
which sparks white on black
across the old onion field,
the steeple will grow high, bright.
We will toast with the chalice of silence.

Helen Lovelock-Burke

Summer Night Piece

The garden is steeped in moonlight,
Full to its high edges with brimming silver,
And the fish-ponds brim and darken
And run in little serpent lights soon extinguished.
Lily-pads lie upon the surface, beautiful as the tarnishings on frail old silver,
And the Harvest moon droops heavily out of the sky,
A ripe, white melon, intensely, magnificently, shining.
Your window is orange in the moonlight,
It glows like a lamp before a shrine.
The small, intimate, familiar shrine,
Placed reverently among the bricks
Of a much-loved garden wall.

Amy Lowell

The Pauper

They call thee rich; I deem thee poor;
  Since, if thou darest not use thy store,
But savest only for thine heirs,
The treasure is not thine but theirs.

Lucilius

Sonnet

I could not sleep for thinking of the sky,
The unending sky, with all its million suns
Which turn their planets everlastingly
In nothing, where the fire-haired comet runs.
If I could sail that nothing, I should cross
Silence and emptiness with dark stars passing;
Then, in the darkness, see a point of gloss
Burn to a glow, and glare, and keep amassing,
And rage into a sun with wandering planets,
And drop behind; and then, as I proceed,
See his last light upon his last moon's granites
Die to a dark that would be night indeed:
Night where my soul might sail a million years
In nothing, not even Death, not even tears.

John Masefield

Summer Farm

Straws like tame lightnings lie about the grass
And hang zigzag on hedges. Green as glass
The water in the horse-trough shines.
Nine ducks go wobbling by in two straight lines.

A hen stares at nothing with one eye,
Then picks it up. Out of an empty sky
A swallow falls and, flickering through
The barn, dives up again into the dizzy blue.

I lie, not thinking, in the cool, soft grass,
Afraid of where a thought might take me—as
This grasshopper with placed face
Unfolds his legs and finds himself in space.

Self under self, a pile of selves I stand
Threaded on time, and with metaphysic hand
Lift the farm like a lid and see
Farm within farm, and in the centre, me.

Norman MacCaig

Yes

A smile says: Yes.
A heart says: Blood.
When the rain says: Drink,
The earth says: Mud.

The Kangaroo says: Trampoline.
Giraffes say: Tree.
A bus says: Us.
While a car says: Me.

Lemon trees say: Lemons
A jug says: Lemonade.
The villain says: You're wonderful.
The hero: I'm afraid.

The forest says: Hide and Seek.
The grass says: Green and Grow.
The railway says: Maybe.
The prison says: No.

The millionaire says: Take.
The beggar says: Give.
The soldier cries: Mother!
The baby sings: Live.

The river says: Come with me.
The moon says: Bless.
The stars say: Enjoy the light.
The sun says: Yes.

Adrian Mitchell

Nepalese proverb

banko bāghle nakhāya pani manko bāghle khāncha

It is not the tiger in the forest but the one in the
mind that eats up a man.

Navigating

Let's board a boat, shall we, and then forget the harbour.
We could look back and see nothing, and then wonder:
is it the wind or a current taking us so fast?
Let's wait for dark, and have no oars,
or rudder even, and a bare mast.

Candy Neubert

Two Little Dogs

Two little dogs
Sat by the fire
Over a fender of coal-dust:
Said one little dog
To the other little dog,
If you don't talk, why, I must.

Nursery rhyme

Sod's Law

I'm standing in a rain storm
             waiting for a bus,
when this geezer next to me
             starts to swear and cuss.

"I've waited for forty minutes now
             in all this bloody wevver,
Soon as I light this sodden fag,
             then two'll come togevver."

Pete O'Keefe

Fish and Chips

Remember
sharing their greasy warmth,
sozzled with vinegar,
yesterday's Herald headlines
printed on our fingers,
as we stood in the shelter
not waiting for buses.

Jennie Osborne

Camera Obscura

Spring flowers on a bank
millions of interweaving stars
in the thrown truth of light.

I photograph all the hot lane:
a hopeless technology for what
can only be developed in the heart.

William Oxley

Fragment

. . . He that but once too nearly hears
The music of forefended spheres
Is thenceforth lonely, and for all
His days like one who treads the wall
Of China, and on this hand, sees
Cities and their civilities,
And, on the other, lions . . .

Coventry Patmore

Through frost and snow and sunlight,
Through rain and night and day
I go back to where I come from.
I pass all things, yet stay.

Brian Patten

The answer to this riddle is on page 118

The Beech and the Sapling Oak

For the tender beech and the sapling oak,
That grow by the shadowy rill,
You may cut down both at a single stroke,
You may cut down which you will.

But this you must know, that as long as they grow,
Whatsoever change may be,
You can never teach either oak or beech
To be aught but a greenwood tree.

Thomas Love Peacock

The Rape of the Lock

Love in these labyrinths his slaves detains,
And mighty hearts are held in slender chains.
With hairy sprindges we the birds betray,
Sight lines of hair surprise the finny prey,
Fair tresses man's imperial race insnare,
And beauty draws us with a single hair.

Alexander Pope

'What is our life? It is a play of passion'

Earth is the stage, heaven the spectator is
Who doth behold whoe'er doth act amiss.
The graves that hide us from the parching sun
Are but drawn curtains till the play is done.

Sir Walter Raleigh

Riddle

I watched a beast of the weaponed sex.
He forced, fired by the first of lusts,
Four fountains which refreshed his youth
To shoot our shining in their shaped ways.

A man stood by that said to me:
'That beast, living, will break clods;
torn to tatters, will tie men's hands.'

The answer to this riddle is on page 118

The Road

Does the road wind uphill all the way?
Yes, to the very end.
Will the day's journey take the whole long day?
From the morn to night, my friend.

Christina Rossetti

May the ambitious ever find

May the ambitious ever find
  Success in crowds and noise,
While gentle love does fill my mind
  With silent real joys.

Let conquering kings new triumphs raise,
  And melt in court delights;
Her eyes can give much brighter days,
  Her arms much softer nights.

C. Sackville, Earl of Dorset

Sound, sound the clarion

Sound, sound the clarion, fill the fife!
  To all the sensual world proclaim,
One crowded hour of glorious life
  Is worth an age without a name.

Sir Walter Scott

Out, out, brief candle!
Life's but a walking shadow, a poor player
That struts and frets his hour upon the stage,
And then is heard no more; it is a tale
Told by an idiot, full of sound and fury,
Signifying nothing.

William Shakespeare

Each is given a bag of tools,
a shapeless mass, a book of rules.
And each must fashion, ere life is flown
a stumbling-block, or a stepping-stone.

R. L. Sharpe

Change

While wondering long on certainty
I wondered long on change
My single final certainty is
That certainty will change
Sure as next year's summer
Sure as this year's rain.

Phil Sheardown

Music when soft voices die

Music, when soft voices die,
Vibrates in the memory—
Odours, when sweet violets sicken,
Live within the sense they quicken.

Rose leaves, when the rose is dead,
Are heap'd for the beloved's bed;
And so thy thoughts, when they are gone,
Love itself shall slumber on.

Percy Bysshe Shelley

'my Cat Jeoffry'

For he purrs in thankfulness, when God tells him he's a good Cat.
For he is an instrument for the children to learn benevolence upon.
For every house is incompleat without him and a blessing is
  lacking in the spirit.

Christopher Smart

Rooks

There, where the rusty iron lies,
   The rooks are cawing all the day,
Perhaps no man, until he dies,
   Will understand them, what they say.

The evening makes the sky like clay.
   The slow wind waits for night to rise.
The world is half-content. But they

Still trouble all the trees with cries,
   That know, and cannot put away,
The yearning to the soul that flies
   From day to night, from night to day.

Charles Sorley

Too late I stayed

Too late I stayed—forgive the crime;
    Unheeded flew the hours;
How noiseless falls the foot of Time,
    That only treads on flowers.

W. R. Spencer

Sindhi Woman

Barefoot through the bazaar,
and with the same undulant grace
as the cloth blown back from her face,
she glides with a stone jar
high on her head
and not a ripple in her tread.

Watching her cross erect
stones, garbage, excrement, and crumbs
of glass in the Karachi slums,
I, with my stoop, reflect
they stand most straight
who learn to walk beneath a weight.

Jon Stallworthy

The Mother

Of course I love them, they are my children.
That is my daughter and this is my son.
And this is my life I give them to please them.
It has never been used. Keep it safe. Pass it on.

Anne Stevenson

The Vagabond

Wealth I ask not; hope nor love,
Nor a friend to know me;
All I ask, the heaven above
And the road below me.

Robert Louis Stevenson

Confidential Moment

The old man sitting behind me
on the bus, leaned forward to say,
"I went with my mother, long ago
to read the gravestones
in the cemetery. On one stone
we read just three words,—*"Learn to die."*
It's what I'm doing now," he said,
and chuckled, very much alive.

Guida Swan

Addenda quaedam

My wife a-rattling,
My children tattling,
My money spent is,
And due my rent is,
My school decreasing,
My income ceasing.
All people tease me,
But no man pays me.

Jonathan Swift

Hail

It attacked me yer honour with its verbals.
Grimy with the sweepings
Of the waiting area of bus stations.
Hung over hills and the other moor dropping its parts—
                                    Column!
Flowering tiny white flowers in the short grass.

Jean Symons

Crossing the Bar

Sunset and evening star,
    And one clear call for me!
And may there be no moaning of the bar,
    When I put out to sea,
But such a tide as moving seems asleep,
    Too full for sound and foam,
When that which drew from out the
    Boundless deep
Turns again home.

Alfred Lord Tennyson

Cock-crow

Out of the wood of thoughts that grows by night
To be cut down by the sharp axe of light,
Out of the night, two cocks together crow,
Cleaving the darkness with a silver blow:
And bright before my eyes twin trumpeters stand,
Heralds of splendour, one at either hand,
Each facing each as in a coat of arms:
The milkers lace their boots up at the farms.

Edward Thomas

The fault is great in man or woman
Who steals a goose from off the common;
But what can plead that man's excuse
Who steals a common from the goose?

from The Tickler Magazine

The Leith police dismisseth us,
  I'm thankful, sir, to say;
The Leith police dismisseth us,
  They thought we sought to stay.
The Leith police dismisseth us,
  We both sighed sighs apiece,
And the sigh that we sighed as we
  said goodbye
Was the size of the Leith police.

Traditional

Star light, star bright,
First star I see tonight,
I wish I may, I wish I might,
Have the wish I wish tonight.

Traditional

Written in the year Chi-hai (879), the first

The submerged country, river and hill, is a battle-ground.
How can the common people enjoy their wood-cutting
  and their fuel-gathering?
I charge thee, sir, not to talk of high honours;
A single general achieves fame on the rotting bones of
  ten thousand.

Ts'ao Sung

Though somewhat late

Though somewhat late, at last I found the way
To leave the doubtful labyrinth of love,
Wherein, alas, each minute seemed a day:
I was enforced, till Reason taught my mind
To slay the beast, and leave him there behind.

Thomas Watson

Insomnia

I love the beauty of the first quarter
and the stillness of my wife
as she breathes like a reclining sea.
I love the sound of my children
lengthening under winter blankets.
And those moments, when on the edge of sleep,
my mind and my fridge
duet with one note.

Darran Whatmore

You who will read this fickle page
Illustrated by the sun,
Scribbled by the shower's rage,
Altering as the minutes run;
Think how alteration must
All endeavours bring to dust,
All that's mortal, man and house,
And of mercy pray for us.

Laurence Whistler

Animals

I think I could turn and live with animals, they are so placid and
      self-contained;
I stand and look at them long and long.
They do not sweat and whine about their condition;
They do not lie awake in the dark and weep for their sins;
They do not make me sick discussing their duty to God;
Not one is dissatisfied—not one is demented with the mania of
      owning things;
Not one kneels to another, nor to his kind that lived thousands of
      years ago;
Not one is respectable or industrious over the whole earth.

Walt Whitman

We flatter those we scarcely know,
We please the fleeting guest,
And deal full many a thoughtless blow
To those who love us best.

Ella Wheeler Wilcox

'That Vain Animal'

Were I, (who to my cost already am,
One of those strange, prodigious Creatures *Man*),
A spirit free, to choose for my own share
What case of Flesh, and Blood, I pleas'd to weare,
I'd be a *Dog*, a *Monkey*, or a *Bear*
Or any thing, but that vain Animal,
Who is so proud of being rational.

John Wilmot, Earl of Rochester

Hence, in a season of calm weather
Though inland far we be,
Our souls have sight of that immortal sea
Which brought us hither;
Can in a moment travel thither—
And see the children sport upon the shore,
And hear the mighty waters rolling evermore.

William Wordsworth

Ballade

They flee from me that sometime did me seek
With naked foot stalking in my chamber.
I have seen them gentle, tame, and meek
That now are wild and do not remember
That sometime they put themselfes in danger
To take bread at my hand; and now they range
Busily seeking with a continual change.

Thomas Wyatt

Notes and acknowledgements

An asterisk indicates poems selected from submissions by members of the public.

Apollinaire, Guillaume (1880–1918): from 'The Little Car', written at the end of the First World War (translated by Ron Padget)

Ariston: 'Mice and Books' (translated by Viola Gerard Garvin)

Arnold, Matthew (1822–1888): 'Below the surface-stream'

Bede, The Venerable: 'The Life of Man', from the Venerable Bede's *Ecclesiastical History of Britain* (c.673–735)

Belsey, Valerie: © 'Catshapes'

Blake, William (1757–1827): 'When a man has married a wife, he finds out whether', from 'Selected Aphorisms and Epigrams', from *Selected Poems* edited by H. Bateson, 1957

Brontë, Charlotte (1816–1855): From 'Stanzas'

Brooke, Rupert (1887–1915): from 'In Freiburg Station'

Buhse, Carola: © 'Seascape'*

Burge, Anthony: © 'Hornbill'*

Burns, Robert (1759–1796): 'On Rough Roads'

Cawein, Madison (1865–1914): 'Song of the road'

Clare, John (1793–1864): 'Song'

Clarke, Valerie: © 'Van Gogh'*

Coleridge, Samuel Taylor (1772–1834): from 'Work without Hope'

Constable, John (1776–1837): 'There is nothing ugly'

Cook, Rose: 'Buffalo'*

Cowper, William (1731–1800): from 'The Solitude of Alexander Selkirk', (who was thought to be the model for Robinson Crusoe)

Crease, Pauline: © 'Marble Arch'*

Daniel, John: © 'Journey'*

Dhammapada: 'Few among men' from *What the Buddha Taught*, translated by Walpola Rahula, published by Gordon Fraser, 1959

Dickinson, Emily (1830–1886): 'Exultation'

Eglinton, Edna: © 'Frosty Night'*

Farnsworth, David: © 'Kettle'*

Ferguson, Gus: © 'Love amongst the Middle-aged', with thanks to the author

Flecker, James Elroy (1884–1915): *'Tenebris Interlucenem'* (From darkness into light)

Folk song: from the folk song known as 'The Cherry Song', *The Oxford Nursery Rhyme Book*, Clarendon, 1955

Ford, John (1586–1639): 'All life is but a wandering'

Freistadt, Berta R.: © 'Everything is hidden'*

Gabon pygmy poem: from 'Ghosts and Shadows', taken from *Technicians of the Sacred, Poetry from Africa, America, Asia and Oceania*

Galton-Fenzi, Jenny: © 'Park and Ride'*

Goldoni, Carlo (1707–1793): 'He who never leaves his country', from 'Pamela'

Goodyer, Ronnie: © 'She clicks the keys of the morning'*

Gray, Thomas (1716–1771): from 'Ode on a Favourite Cat, Drowned in a Tub of Gold Fishes'

Grillus: from the Greek, translator unknown

Hardy, Thomas (1840–1928): 'The Garden Seat'

Harington, Sir J. (1561–1612): 'Against writers that carp against other men's books'

Harvey, Matt: 'Such Bus as Dreams are Made of', from 'Here we are then'

Hay, John Milton: 'Distich'

Herrick, Robert (1591–1674): 'Discontents'

Hood, Thomas (1799–1845): from 'I remember, I remember'

Japanese saying: (author unknown) from *The Vagabond Path: an anthology* edited by Iris Origo

Jimenez, Juan Ramon: © from *'Tarde andaluza'* (Andalucian afternoon), number 17 of a sequence of poems entitled *'En Tren'* (In the Train), translated by Valerie Belsey. From *Collected Poems* published by Aguilar, Madrid.

Jonson, Ben (1573–1637): from his play *The Silent Woman*, 1609.

Keats, John (1795–1821): 'Dawlish Fair'

Kirby, Angela: © 'Eagle'*

Lawrence, D. H. (1885–1930): 'Ultimate reality'

Leapor, Mary (1722–1746): from 'The Enquiry'

Leonidas of Tarentum: 'The Roadside Pool' from *The Open Road, A Little Book for Wayfarers* compiled by E. V. Lucas, Methuen and Co., 1905

Lord Byron, George Gordon (1788–1824): 'Pathless Woods'

Lovelock-Burke, Helen: © 'Steeple'*

Lowell, Amy (1874–1925): 'Summer night'

Lucilius: 'The Pauper', translated by William Cowper

Masefield, John (1878–1967): © 'Sonnet V', with thanks to the Society of Authors as the literary representative of the Estate of John Masefield

MacCaig, Norman (1910–1996): © 'Summer Farm', with thanks to Chatto and Windus

Mitchell, Adrian: (b.1932) © 'Yes' with thanks to the author. Published in *Blue Coffee* (Bloodaxe Books) and *Balloon Lagoon* (Orchard Books, 96, Leonard Street, London EC2)

Nepalese proverb: from *Proverbs and Sayings from Nepal* collected by Ratna Pustak Bhandar, 1994, translated by Kesar Lall

Neubert, Candy: © 'Navigating'

Nursery rhyme: '2 little dogs' from *The Oxford Nursery Rhyme Book*, Clarendon Press, 1955

O'Keefe, Pete: © 'Sod's Law'*

Osborne, Jennie: © 'Fish 'n' chips'*

Oxley, William: © 'Camera Obscura'*

Patmore, Coventry (1823–1896): 'A Fragment'

Peacock, Thomas Love (1785–1866): from 'The Beech and the Sapling Oak' (from the novel *Maid Marian*).

Patten, Brian: © 'Through frost and snow' from *The New Exeter Book of Riddles*, edited by Kevin Crossley-Holland and Lawrence Sail, Enitharmon Press 1999

Pope, Alexander (1688–1744): from 'The Rape of the Lock'

Raleigh, Walter (1552–1618): From 'What is our life?'

Saxon Riddle: 'Bullock' from *The Earliest English Poems* translated by Michael Alexander, Penguin Classic, 1966

Rossetti, Christina (1830–1894): from 'The Road'

Sackville, Charles Earl of Dorset (1638–1706): 'May the ambitious ever find'

Scott, Sir Walter (1771–1832): 'Sound, sound the clarion' from 'Old Mortality'

Shakespeare, William (1564–1616): 'Out, out brief candle . . .' from Macbeth's speech in Act V Scene V.

Sharpe, R. L. : 'Bag of tools' (no biographical data available)

Sheardown, Phil: © 'Change'*

Shelley, Percy Bysshe (1792–1822): 'Music when soft voices die'

Smart, Christopher (1722–1771): from 'my Cat Jeoffry'

Sorley, Charles (1895–1915): 'Rooks'

Spencer, W. R. (1769–1834): from 'Too late I stayed'

Stallworthy, Jon: 'Sindhi Woman' from *Rounding the Horn: Collected Poems* (CarcanetUK)

Stevenson, Anne (b. 1933): © 'The Mother', with thanks to the author

Stevenson, Robert Louis (1850–1894): from 'The Vagabond' (set to music by R. Vaughan Williams)

Swan, Guida: © 'Confidential Moment'*

Swift, Jonathan (1667–1745): '*Addenda quaedam*' ('In addition to this')

Symons, Jean: © 'Hail'*

Tennyson, Alfred Lord (1809–1892): from 'Crossing the Bar'

Thomas, Edward (1878–1917): 'Cock-crow'

The Tickler Magazine, 1821 ('The fault is great in man or woman')

Watson, Thomas (1557–1592): 'Though somewhat late'

Whatmore, Darran: © 'Insomnia'*

Whistler, Laurence: "This rhyme was scratched by the famous painter on the glass of a garden door in Oxford" (Henry Williamson made a note of this when he edited the volume entitled *Norfolk Life*, written by Lilias Rider Haggard in 1943)

Whitman, Walt (1819–1892): from 'Animals'

Wilcox, Ella Wheeler (1850–1919): 'We flatter those we scarcely know'

Wilmot John, Earl of Rochester (1647–1680): from 'The Vain Animal'

Wordsworth, William (1770–1850): from 'Ode on Intimations of Immortality from Recollections of Early Childhood'

Wyatt, Sir Thomas (1503–42): from 'They flee from me that sometime did me seek' (*Vixi Puellis Nuper Idoneus*), Ballade LXXX

Answers to riddles:

page 78: signpost

page 82: bullock

Index of first lines